Towards a universal upper secondary education system in England

A unified and ecosystem vision

Ann Hodgson and Ken Spours

Professors of Education

Based on an Inaugural Professorial Lecture delivered at the Institute of Education, University of London, on 27 June 2012

Institute of Education, University of London
Professorial Lecture Series

Leading education and social research
Institute of Education
University of London

First published in 2012 by the Institute of Education, University of London,
20 Bedford Way, London WC1H 0AL
www.ioe.ac.uk/publications

British Library Cataloguing in Publication Data:
A catalogue record for this publication is available from the British Library

ISBN 978 0 85473 923 3

Typeset by Quadrant Infotech (India) Pvt Ltd

Printed by ImageData Group

Towards a universal upper secondary education system in England

Ann Hodgson and Ken Spours

Biography

Ann Hodgson has worked as a teacher, lecturer, LEA adviser, editor and civil servant, joining the Institute of Education, University of London in 1993, where she is now a Professor of Education, Assistant Director (London) and Co-director of the Centre for Post-14 Research and Innovation. Ann supervises a large number of doctoral students and teaches on a range of masters and doctoral courses. She has recently co-directed a major three-year ESRC-funded project, on the impact of policy on teaching, learning and assessment in the learning and skills sector, and also the six-year Nuffield Review of 14–19 Education and Training in England and Wales. Her current projects include A Partnership Approach to 14–19 Progression and Transition in North East Lincolnshire; Global Learning for Global Colleges, funded by the Department for International Development; work on professional learning with the Institute for Learning; acting as an academic partner for London councils on 14–19 education and training; and a survey with the NUT and UCU on teacher and lecturer views of 14–19 policy. Ann has published widely in a variety of forms on topics related to post-14 education policy, vocational education and training, lifelong learning, and curriculum and qualifications reform. Recent books include: *Post-compulsory education and lifelong learning across the United Kingdom: Policy, organisation and governance* (IOE Publications, 2011), co-edited with Ken Spours and Martyn Waring; *Education for all: The future of education and training for 14–19 year olds* (Routledge, 2009), co-authored with other Nuffield Review directors and researchers; *Education and training 14–19: Curriculum, qualifications and organisation* (Sage, 2008), co-authored with Ken Spours; and *Improving Learning, Skills and Inclusion: The impact of policy on post-compulsory education* (Routledge, 2008), co-authored with Frank Coffield, Sheila Edward, Ian Finlay, Ken Spours and Richard Steer.

Biography

Ken Spours is an Assistant Director for Equalities and Engagement at the Institute of Education, University of London. He is co-Director of the Centre for Post-14 Research and Innovation. He specializes in research on post-14 curriculum and qualifications, organisation and governance, and learner progression and transitions. He also undertakes research on education and training developments across the four countries of the UK.

Ken was a member of the Tomlinson Working Group on 14–19 Reform and a director of the Nuffield Review of 14–19 Education and Training in England and Wales. He is presently convenor of the Compass (Direction for the Democratic Left) Education Group.

Recent publications include: *Education for the Good Society*, edited with Neal Lawson (Compass Publications, 2011); 'Democratic localism', in *Soundings* vol. 49 (Winter 2011); *Post-compulsory education and lifelong learning across the UK: policy, organisation and governance* (IOE Publications, 2011) co-edited with Ann Hodgson and Martyn Waring; *Education for all: the future of education and training for 14–19 year olds* (Routledge, 2009), co-authored with other Nuffield Review directors and researchers; and *Education and Training 14–19: Curriculum, qualifications and organisation* (Sage, 2008), co-authored with Ann Hodgson.

Towards a universal upper secondary education system in England: A unified and ecosystem vision

Is it now appropriate to talk about an upper secondary education[1] system in England?[2] The term 'upper secondary' is more commonly used at the international level when describing the phase that precedes higher education or entry to the labour market. We think it is useful to use this term and, moreover, to argue for a *universal* upper secondary education system. Thinking about the education of 14–19-year-olds in this way brings considerable demands and requires a new form of critical analysis. Currently upper secondary education in England remains a truncated experience for many, often with little extra to show for any additional years of study beyond 16, and without significantly better employment prospects.[3] Moreover, it is a set of arrangements, rather than a system as such. The underlying assumption of this lecture is that England needs to develop a universal upper secondary education system that develops the potential of all, enhances the life chances of young people and goes well beyond the aim of current government policy to raise the participation age to 18 by 2015.

Our vision of a universal upper secondary education system is explored through a discussion of two related concepts: first, a more 'unified' 14–19 phase that addresses head-on the academic/vocational divide and, second, an 'ecosystem' approach to reform that links changes in the curriculum and qualifications to a range of other factors – organisational, social, political and economic – at national, regional and local levels.

In the current global and national economic context we suggest that policy-makers face three options for education reform: to work within the existing historical compromises, to move to more explicitly divided arrangements or to build a new, more inclusive and unified system. In our view, the first and second will simply reproduce deep historical problems and only the third option has the potential to address what we see as the major challenges for 14–19 education in England – inadequate performance, lack of equity for different groups of young people and a weak relationship between education, the economy and the democratic process in this country.

The concept of unification runs through the lecture. You might have noticed that there are two of us on the platform. This is not common practice for a professorial inaugural lecture at the Institute of Education, University of London (IOE), or anywhere else as far as we know. So we feel the need to offer an explanation. We deeply believe in collaborative work because we know from experience that dialogue produces the best outcomes. We also acknowledge the wide range of contributions to the debate about 14–19 education and training that we will attempt to bring together in this lecture. The vision presented here tonight is the product of a 20-year partnership in which we have worked together for the transformation of upper secondary education in England. However, we are not identical in what we think or how we might express ideas, nor is unification about making everything the same; rather it is about celebrating diversity within a sense of common purpose. Unified does not mean uniform.

Reflecting on events and our work over the past two decades, we realise that it is no easy task to argue for a unified upper secondary system and there are good reasons why we have failed in the past. We also have to take account of the challenges of the new economic and political context since 2008. Here we will argue for a 'serious utopianism'[4] that is grounded in current conditions, exercises 'policy memory',[5] appreciates the strengths as well as tackles the weaknesses of English 14–19 education and training, and recognises what we refer to as an 'ecological' interrelationship between the different elements of reform – aims and purposes, curriculum and qualifications, organisational arrangements, the economy and the labour market, professional capacity and the reform process itself. Finally, we have to find a way of capturing the public imagination with a vision of what it is to develop an 'educated 19-year-old',[6] capable of innovative thinking and doing, entrepreneurship, civic participation and collaboration in a diverse society and globalised world. As Frank Coffield and Bill Williamson remind us, schools and colleges need to be much more than 'examination factories'.[7]

We assert that the upper secondary education system in England should reflect and promote the more equal and democratic society that we want to build rather than reinforce its current inequalities and divisions. We want to foster a sense of optimism for young people, for those who work with them and for society at large about the power of education to transform lives at a time of deepening crisis in the economy, the environment and social relations. Our lecture is a small contribution to this end.

The contested case of 14–19 education and training

For some time upper secondary education in England has been the focus of social and political contestation, but this has intensified as a result of pressure from the new economic and political context. The official concept of a 14–19 phase is a relatively recent development, starting with New Labour's 2002 Green Paper,[8] and facing an uncertain future since the election of a Conservative-led Coalition Government in 2010. Despite the fact that it is now no longer policy 'flavour of the month', there are still strong arguments for a holistic and comprehensive 14–19 phase. Three stand out. The first concerns an explicit recognition of a period when young people are making the transition to adulthood and where it is necessary to have a curriculum that acknowledges this process.[9] Second, there are a series of practical reasons why a longitudinal approach makes sense. The choices young people make at 14 affect their options at 16 and beyond. To ensure effective progression from 14–16 and post-16, the qualifications that primarily shape the curriculum for 14–19-year-olds need to be closely aligned and time must be allowed for their completion. Some learners will take longer than others. Upper secondary education is also a time when young people begin to specialise in their study, which raises questions about the balance between breadth and depth over this phase. The third set of arguments concerns the wider social and economic implications of upper secondary education. It has become the focus of social contestation and the point at which selection takes place because this is where young people's future life chances are increasingly determined.[10] It is no surprise that developed (and now developing) countries consider the performance of upper secondary education as economically and socially important. For this reason, even if the current government does not explicitly recognise the existence of a '14–19 phase', education professionals and the wider public should.

Despite these arguments for a longitudinal approach to upper secondary education, the discontinuities between the 14–16 and 16–19 phases remain powerful and have been strengthened by recent policy. The idea of 14–19 education is thus relatively fragile. Moreover, this fragility is reinforced by a pervasive sense of discontent. Few appear happy with the current arrangements. Every August brings hand-wringing about slipping standards as more learners pass GCSEs and A Levels. Employers complain that young people are not ready for working life. Universities moan that it is impossible to distinguish between candidates with high A Level scores. Successive governments lament the low position of the English education system within international league tables. Sixth form tutors claim that the students they receive do not have the skills or knowledge to successfully undertake A Levels, and colleges assert that some 16-year-olds are not adequately prepared for specialist vocational courses. Many young people are not happy either. Their dissatisfaction is not so much with the education they receive (satisfaction rates remain high[11]) as with their prospects at the end of the phase, given the high numbers of those unable to find a job.[12]

At the root of this dissatisfaction lies a lack of settled will about the aims of English upper secondary education. Is its dominant purpose meritocratic – that is, to select the highest-attaining young people for university and the best jobs? Or is its primary purpose a democratic one – that is, to provide all young people with a broad preparation for working and adult life, with the aim of also creating new opportunities? These crucial issues, despite successive waves of reform in recent years, have not been sufficiently debated,[13] because upper secondary education in England has crept up on us almost by default as a result of changes to the youth labour market, rising social aspirations and incremental reform of qualifications. In policy terms, the 14–19 phase is both new and has developed in a haphazard way. It differs from earlier phases, such as primary education, where there is a consensus about its universality and purpose. These issues of purpose and consensus with regard to upper secondary education have become more acute as we move towards 2015 and the raising of the participation age to 18, which *de facto* suggests some sort of universality. In this lecture we will argue for the second of these purposes – democratic – but we will also suggest that history and policy have gone with the first – selection.

In an era of neo-liberalism, education has been seen as the main way for individuals to get ahead in what Phil Brown and colleagues refer to as the 'global auction' of international talent.[14] Individual performance becomes the be-all and end-all in a race to gain places at the most prestigious universities and access to high-status jobs. This system of winners and losers in part explains why, despite material progress in the provision of education over the last thirty years, there has been a gradual loss of optimism about the role that it can play in improving society and bringing about change in the human condition.[15]

Nowhere is this more starkly illustrated than in upper secondary education. While we recognise that inequality in educational opportunities starts before schooling begins,[16] it is in the 14–19 phase that division characterises the system. Effectively, the age at which selection takes place has moved from 11+ to 16+. Through the combined effects of different qualification routes, the role of selective schools/colleges and inequalities in funding, this phase has become the crucible in which the life chances of young people are forged.

Divisive expansion and the 'low-opportunity-progression equilibrium'

Looked at historically, the development of an upper secondary phase in England could be seen as a form of 'divisive expansion'. National education systems – state-led with either strong education- or work-based routes – topped the charts in post-compulsory participation in the late 1970s and early 1980s.[17] England's 'mixed' upper secondary system compared badly with its European counterparts.[18] By the mid-1980s the pressures to expand were proving irresistible. The question was: which type of upper secondary system would lead to expansion? What followed were debates about its essential features – should it become a dual system like Germany, Austria and Switzerland or take a more unified approach like France or Scotland?[19] In the event, neither of these transpired. Instead, what emerged was a typically English compromise – a complex triple-track qualifications system underpinned by competitive and mixed institutional arrangements. This fragmented formation has failed to deliver the high-participation/high-achievement system to which successive governments have aspired. A fundamental reappraisal is needed.

In their seminal 1988 article on the problems of post-compulsory education and training, David Finegold and David Soskice argued that Britain was trapped in a 'low-skills equilibrium' – a syndrome of systemic factors preventing the creation of a high-skills approach to economic development.[20] A great deal has changed since, notably the near doubling of the numbers of young people staying on in education after 16. However, despite this expansion, we will suggest that the low-skills equilibrium continues in a new form. Education and training for 14–19-year-olds suffers from a negatively reinforcing set of systemic factors to create what we term a 'low-opportunity-progression equilibrium'. While more young people than ever stay on at 16, many do not develop the knowledge or skills to progress further in a highly selective system. Too many leave at 17+ and, at the end of the phase, the prospect of unemployment or underemployment looms.[21] Those at risk are not only the most excluded – those young people known as NEETs (Not in Education, Employment or Training) – but also a group that has been referred to as the 'overlooked middle'.[22] These include those young people on lower-level post-16 courses who have not been able to access either the A Level royal route to the most prestigious universities or the most sought-after apprenticeships. In an economic environment now short on opportunity and with a government committed to a traditional curriculum and overseeing a chronically weak work-based route, these young people risk becoming the new NEETs.

The fact that 14–19 education is trapped in this static equilibrium is the result of a set of factors that have been consolidated despite thirty years of political tinkering: continuing divided curriculum and qualifications arrangements, school sixth forms and sixth form colleges competing for the highest-attaining students and ignoring others, the disempowerment of teachers and lecturers that frustrates the development of a deeper professionalism,[23] the overbearing role of selective universities in 14–19 education, coupled with what Ewart Keep refers to as the 'mysterious absence of employers'.[24] All of these have been compounded by a policy process in which ministers have tended to treat education as a 'political football'. The result is a 14–19 phase that is stuck fast, with division and inequity contributing to the underperformance of all learners, but particularly the overlooked middle and the NEETs. It also seems to be relatively incapable of promoting a plausible narrative about developing the knowledge and skills needed for a better future.

Five dimensions of a low-opportunity-progression equilibrium

The complex upper secondary education and training arrangements that emerged in the mid-1990s basically remain with us to the present day. Moreover, we suggest that the low-opportunity-progression equilibrium is now intensifying because of the impact of five dimensions that produce a 'cancelling effect'; a process of reform that, like a 'tethered beetle', is destined to follow the same circular path without moving forward.[25]

A divided qualifications system

The system is still dominated by GCSEs and A Levels, and vocational education fails to flourish. New Labour's Curriculum 2000 reforms, while opening up access to A Level attainment, also led to learner instrumentalism as they focused on examination technique and resitting modules to achieve three good A Level grades, rather than on developing the wider skills required for higher study.[26] Even the highest-attaining students, unlike their European counterparts, are not actively encouraged to engage with the broader purposes of education nor to acquire the skills and knowledge required for a rapidly changing world.[27] A Levels also continue to cast a long shadow over other awards. New qualifications, such as General National Vocational Qualifications, Advanced Certificates of Vocational Education and the 14–19 Diplomas, sought to offer something more applied, but ended up aping A Levels in a search for 'parity of esteem', becoming neither strongly general nor strongly vocational.[28] The result has been a narrow, dominant academic curriculum and a weak, low-status vocational education.

Secretary of State Michael Gove's reforms of GCSE and vocational qualifications are but another circumnavigation of this tethered beetle. The English Baccalaureate performance measure,[29] with its emphasis on traditional subjects and likely to be followed by linear A Levels, is an attempt to reverse the mild bureaucratic broadening and accessibility of general education undertaken by New Labour. The risk is that general education will become narrower and failure rates will increase. For those young people excluded from this route, little is actually being done to fundamentally improve the status of vocational education, despite all the heat and light of the Wolf Review.[30]

A competitive mixed economy of providers

Unlike other European systems (or even those in Scotland and Wales), England currently has a complex range of competing providers delivering 14–19 education.[31] Young people and their parents are confronted by a dizzying array of institutions – academies, maintained 11–16 or 11–18 schools, free schools, university technical colleges, studio schools, sixth form colleges, general further education colleges, independent learning providers, employers – but their actual degree of choice depends on a learner's level of attainment and the institutional arrangements in the locality. Many students do not choose; they are chosen. High-attaining learners following the A Level route usually have little to worry about. Competitive choice-based arrangements, however, impact negatively on the 'overlooked middle'. Schools with sixth forms have a strong incentive to advise their Year 11 students to remain in the school beyond 16 and little reason to recommend apprenticeships or vocational courses that reduce sixth form numbers (and funding). The consequent lack of impartial information, advice and guidance (IAG) increases the possibility that young people will be placed on A Level courses, because these are the easiest for schools to deliver given their staffing. In addition, they are high status and popular with parents. Students are therefore encouraged to take courses with which they may struggle, with the risk of dropping out at 17+. Moreover, across an area, the logic of institutional self-interest leads to the over-provision of some courses (A Levels) and the under-provision of others (Level 1 and Level 2 vocational qualifications). Resources thus become inequitably distributed in favour of the more advantaged students, and inefficiencies occur. Even A Level choice shrinks as small school sixth forms offer the same 'popular' subjects and are unable to provide minority options, such as languages. Vocational provision also suffers because of a lack of critical mass, and expensive vocational resources can remain underutilised. As Geoff Stanton and Mick Fletcher put it, greater institutional diversity leads to less curriculum choice.[32]

The role of employers and higher education: ghosts and elephants

To the mutually reinforcing role of curriculum and organisation can be added the influence of end-users – employers and higher education. Employers' participation in education and training can be likened to a ghost – although invited to contribute, they are at best a shadow sitting at the table. Meanwhile, higher education is the elephant in the room – of such huge significance that no one actually appears to notice it.

Successive governments have accorded employers a privileged voice in upper secondary education, hoping to persuade them to contribute. However, they continue to be a reluctant social partner, despite islands of excellent practice. The offer of apprenticeships for young people remains very low, involving around 6 per cent of 16–18-year-olds nationally, and any growth in this area is often a rebadging exercise involving, for example, ASDA and Morrisons using apprenticeship funds to train their own 50-year-old staff.[33] Moreover, utilisation of skills by employers remains underdeveloped.[34] Here the wider effects of economic policy are also felt: poor growth rates, low incentives to train and strong incentives to cut costs.

The presence of higher education, on the other hand, is all too real. It exercises a huge influence over A Levels and has repeatedly frustrated reform.[35] Because of its preference for narrow forms of specialisation, in the case of the Russell Group universities, or recruitment at any price among some of the post-1992 institutions, higher education has rarely spoken out clearly in favour of breadth in the 14–19 curriculum. Instead, the prevailing message is still one of grade acquisition in three subjects. This does not mean that higher education tutors are happy with the outcomes of upper secondary education,[36] but they seem powerless to voice their concerns in a coherent or progressive way.

Teacher professionalism and the reform process

The final two systemic factors are linked in a perverse relationship. Education professionals working in competitive institutions have, for the past 20 years, been the objects of policy levers (e.g. targets, funding, inspection, performance measures and national benchmarks)[37] that produce their own cancelling effects. Every useful policy initiative – a graduate profession, better pay, Teach First, the emphasis on teaching and learning – has been negated by a countervailing factor – having to work within a narrow curriculum and assessment system, constant bureaucracy and change, an Ofsted regime that sways in the wind of national politics and the general feeling by the profession that despite all their efforts, nothing they do is right.[38] Education professionals have thus found themselves in a politicised policy process in which successive governments have sought to redefine their professionalism from above. Sounding tough, it is calculated, will deliver political benefits. What is missing in a renewed adversarial climate is the time and space for teacher and lecturer collaboration to develop a deeper, more articulate and more trusted professionalism and the stability to be able to focus on teaching and learning.[39]

Summary – turbulence without change

These five factors work together to undermine both general and vocational education. Rooted in selection and division, they have produced a stasis that, while internally highly active and dynamic, cannot seem to move to a new condition that would produce beneficial outcomes for the 14–19 cohort as a whole. They also generate widespread discontent, mainly among end-users of the system who remain unconvinced that increases in measured attainment have been matched by real increases in knowledge and skills. Students, while remaining remarkably sanguine about their educational experience, worry about their prospects.[40] What we have termed a 'low-opportunity-progression equilibrium' is not the result of complacency. There have been quantitative changes in participation and attainment, not least because of the huge efforts made by students, teachers, lecturers, schools and colleges. These have been undermined, however, by repeated national reforms that fail to address the root causes that frustrate the progression of learners and their transition to higher study and the workplace. A new approach is called for that builds on the genuine strengths of the 14–19 phase and addresses its deeper, and often historical, failings. But first we must learn from history and exercise what Jeremy Higham and David Yeomans have referred to as 'policy memory'[41] in order to engage in policy learning. Radical change is a difficult process that demands reflection.

Policy memory and policy learning – understanding why reforms fail

The historic failure to achieve real change is best reflected in the case of the totemic A Levels. Almost immediately after these qualifications were introduced in 1951, concerns were raised about what was considered to be an excessively specialised and academic curriculum as well as about the relevance of A Levels to the country's future economic and social needs.[42] These criticisms continued throughout the latter half of the twentieth century, with several attempts by official government committees, awarding bodies and others to reform the curriculum and qualifications system for 16–19-year-olds, although they were always successfully rebuffed by conservative forces.[43] If anything, the clamour for reform grew louder as the millennium approached, with the publication of *A British Baccalaureate* in 1990;[44] an official review by Sir Ron Dearing in 1996;[45] and a plethora of proposals from teacher unions and professional associations, learned bodies, opposition political parties and other civil society organisations.[46] However, this was not enough to persuade New Labour to be radical in the late 1990s. Instead, they settled for a number of half measures.

The beginning of this century brought in the Curriculum 2000 reforms, which changed the internal shape of 16–19 qualifications, but did little to stem the tide of criticism about the narrowness of advanced level study and the weakness of vocational education in the upper secondary phase.[47] The problem with the Curriculum 2000 reforms was that they were a bureaucratic and technical compromise to encourage greater accessibility and breadth of study in A Levels, to raise the status of vocational qualifications and to introduce key skills, but without the support of the full baccalaureate framework that had been recommended by the Labour Party itself in 1996.[48] In terms of breadth Curriculum 2000 failed to make a significant difference. Largely due to the influence of higher education institutions' admissions requirements, students ended up typically taking four AS levels in their first year of advanced level study and three in their second year.[49] The Curriculum 2000 reforms made A Levels more accessible through modularisation and the AS/A2 design, but with an approach so mechanical that it has provided the space for a strong Conservative Party counter-argument for quality and deeper learning.[50]

Following problems with the implementation of Curriculum 2000, an alternative approach emerged in 2003–04 in the form of the Tomlinson Committee's proposal for a unified and inclusive 14–19 Diploma system encompassing all forms of study. Despite gaining widespread support, this was rejected by Prime Minister Tony Blair in late 2004 on the political grounds that it threatened A Levels. Looking back, however, the reasons for the failure of the Tomlinson Report lay not only with New Labour politics, but also with the limitations of the proposals themselves. The wider political ground had not been prepared with the public at large, despite a decade of debate within the education profession. In retrospect, it is easy to see how the Tomlinson Report could have been viewed as a 'radical turn' because it was not immediately clear how it was building on the A Level tradition. Prepared in haste and the product of a committee, the proposals became too complicated and difficult to explain. While popular within the profession, everyone had her/his own interpretation of the Report, so the consensus proved superficial. Furthermore, had the unified Diploma system been made policy in late 2004, it would have faced difficulties in implementation. With the benefit of hindsight, the Tomlinson proposals might be regarded as an example of a qualifications-led reform that risked isolation and dilution because they were not supported by wider organisational, labour market, professional and policy change.

Since 2005 aspects of the Tomlinson proposals have re-emerged in more limited forms (e.g. the 14–19 Diplomas,[51] AQA Bacc,[52] SFBac[53] and the Extended Project Qualification[54]). Their partial incorporation into a divided qualifications system has proved to be problematic because they are now associated with failure (the ill-fated 14–19 Diplomas), something that is additional and a possible burden (the AQA Bacc or SFBac frameworks) or underpowered (the Extended Project Qualification). Both New Labour and now the Coalition Government have flirted with diplomas and baccalaureates, but these have either failed (the 14–19 Diplomas) or promise a new divisiveness (Michael Gove's EBacc and Centre Forum's proposal for an A Level Bac[55]).

So what lessons can we learn from recent history? First, be clear why reform is necessary and of your overarching purposes. Second, be prepared to tackle the dominant tradition (in the English case, A Levels), while demonstrating that you are building on its strengths and addressing its weaknesses. Third, resist bureaucratic half-measures – they rarely ever work and tend to alienate. Fourth, realise that successful change requires a combination of vision and the patience to prepare the ground carefully. Finally, curriculum and qualifications reform has to be reinforced by wider measures.

Challenges of the new context – intensifying the low-opportunity-progression equilibrium

While we have to be aware of the roots of historic failures to reform, we also need to recognise the challenges of the new context that is transforming the landscape for upper secondary education in England: the ongoing recession and the education policies of the current Coalition Government. Mass unemployment among 18–25-year-olds, coupled with austerity measures affecting the public and private sectors, threatens to intensify the low-opportunity-progression equilibrium.

The dynamics of the new crisis can be dissected using David Raffe's participation 'push' and 'pull' factors,[56] which affect young people's decisions to remain in education beyond the official leaving age. We identify five potential 'push' factors – legislation; an accessible and motivational curriculum; collaboration between education institutions to offer a wide range of provision in a locality; high-quality careers education, information, advice and guidance (CEIAG); and financial rewards. It is possible to argue that while current government policy supports the first of these, through its statutory commitment to the raising of the participation age,[57] the same cannot be said of the other four. Changes to 14–19 curriculum and qualifications policy, with the introduction of the EBacc performance measure and a greater emphasis on schools offering traditional GCSEs at Key Stage 4, could result in more young people failing to gain adequate qualifications to progress to advanced level study at 16+. An emphasis on institutional diversity and competition rather than collaboration and partnership, as we have seen earlier, is likely to reduce curriculum choice across a locality, with particularly adverse effects for learners progressing to vocational programmes and lower-level post-16 courses. The 2011 Education Act's changes to the provision of CEIAG – so that this becomes the responsibility of individual schools rather than of an independent external agency – raises further questions about impartiality. Finally, the replacement of the Education Maintenance Allowance (EMA) for 16–19-year-olds by a lower level of targeted funding risks reducing the number of young people willing or able to participate effectively in post-16 education.

The picture grows bleaker still when the three major 'pull' factors – access to higher education, entry to a coveted apprenticeship place or getting a good job – are considered. Policies to increase and widen access to higher education over the past 20 years have undoubtedly brought a university education within the reach of substantial numbers of young people and have encouraged many to stay on in school or college to gain the necessary qualifications. However, the sudden hike in higher education fees from September 2012 already appears to be making this option less attractive to young people,[58] many of whom fear the level of debt they will be saddled with when they leave university, particularly in an uncertain labour market. High-quality apprenticeship places, despite successive governments' best efforts, are not available in large numbers for 16–19-year-olds and in the current economic climate this situation is unlikely to change. Perhaps of most concern are the depressingly high unemployment figures for 18–25-year-olds in England. The promise of staying on in education to gain the qualifications that lead to a good job has, as Philip Brown and colleagues argue eloquently in *The Global Auction*,[59] been well and truly broken.

If this is the case, we, in common with Frank Coffield and Bill Williamson,[60] want to ask whether we should not be considering a new role for education (in this case upper secondary education). Rather than thinking of it primarily as a means of gaining qualifications and building the human capital that politicians of all parties in England have claimed makes us competitive in an increasingly globalised marketplace, should we not also be debating its role in helping us to tackle the major societal problems we face in this country? While many of these are connected with the economy and our future place in the global market, they also relate to the environment, to migration, to social justice, to the effects of devolution within the UK and even to the nature of democracy in the more diverse society that is contemporary Britain. These are the broader concerns, alongside the traditional strengths and weaknesses of English upper secondary education, that underpin our vision of a universal and unified 14–19 system.

Building a universal upper secondary education system in England

The chimera of an English dual system

The pressures of the current context place us at a crossroads. Already the Coalition Government has decided that the way forward is a more explicitly divided system, with a traditional academic general education and a vocational education more oriented to apprenticeship. The sub-text could be interpreted as early tracking at 14+. The messages here, however, are less clear, with the Wolf Report[61] arguing for a broad base of general education up to 16, but with other policies, such as studio schools[62] and university technical colleges,[63] suggesting a greater acceptance of early vocational specialisation.

Can a more explicit dual system in England improve performance and create more opportunities for young people? At first glance it looks like an attractive proposition – a distinctive route with its own status based on a strong relationship with the labour market. Closer scrutiny, however, suggests that this is a chimera in the English context, particularly given current policy preferences. The widening of the academic/vocational divide from 14+ will result, as it always has done, in higher-attaining students choosing academic education and lower-attaining ones finding themselves directed towards the vocational route. Moreover, the type of vocational education on offer risks dilution because of a lack of adequate employer involvement.[64] Instead, the driving force affecting its status will be the previous attainment of students taking it, and the relationship between attainment and social class,[65] not the status effects of association with the labour market.

Post-16, the divisions will intensify because A Levels (particularly in the more restrictive form envisaged by the Coalition Government) will be increasingly attuned to the top selective universities who are only interested in a very small proportion of young people. High-quality apprenticeships, on the other hand, on which a successful dual system depends, will also be relatively scarce because of the current economic context and the Coalition Government's commitment to 'one of the least regulated and therefore most "flexible" labour markets in the developed world'.[66]

The idea of an English dual system featured at the end of the 1980s,[67] but all that resulted in the early 1990s were complex triple-track arrangements. With current policy there is every indication that history will repeat itself, this time with the emergence of two small high-status poles – A Levels and apprenticeships – and a large, low-status middle ground of the broad vocational college-based courses unloved by the government and often unsupported by employers.[68]

Policy memory, as well as contextual awareness, tells us that reform by division is doomed to failure. It is time, once again, for radical thinking – taking expansive approaches to both general and vocational education and reinforcing their connectivity, developing a social partnership approach to apprenticeships that significantly raises their presence in the system, and encouraging new levels of local collaboration that engage employers far more closely with education. These strategies, we will argue below, are not based on duality, but on unification, integration and connection, in which vocational education becomes mainstream and, therefore, attractive to all sections of the 14–19 cohort. Our contention is that young people should be engaged in different ways in both types of activity.

The alternative – a unified and ecosystem approach

We will now suggest that the static equilibrium in the 14–19 phase has to be superseded by a new type of system dynamic in order to build a universal upper secondary education system. Here we try to connect two ideas: first, the concept of unification that supports the development of broad underlying capacities in all learners, but can also respond to the different needs of young people as they increasingly specialise; and second, the concept of 'ecosystems' that appreciates the interdependence of a wide range of factors required for successful reform.

The notion of 'unified' is not about uniformity and 'one size fits all'. In exploring unification in relation to what young people learn and achieve – curriculum and qualifications – we will argue that any form of specialisation should involve a strong relationship between the practical and theoretical, regardless of previous levels of attainment. Relating thinking and doing is inherently human and an upper secondary curriculum for the age in which we live and the future we anticipate should reflect this. We also wish to apply the concept of unification to system-building more broadly. This involves recognising that upper secondary education should be seen as part of a complex and interdependent ecological system that requires collective deliberation and action to promote the sustainable participation, development and progression of all 14–19-year-olds. The concept of unification applied in this way also suggests a dialectical relationship with concepts of diversity – individual need, institutional autonomy and devolution of responsibility.

In building this more unified and dynamic concept of system change we adapt David Finegold's concept of 'high skill ecosystems'[69] (used in his case to describe the relationship between clusters of high-tech companies and research-intensive universities in California) to argue for the creation of a national 'high-opportunity-progression ecosystem' (HOPE) for upper secondary education in England that can respond to both the challenges of history and the new context. We will argue that such an ecological approach will require a number of related dimensions of reform that embrace unity and diversity, national and local, leadership and professionalism, change and stability. In this sense, the concepts of unification and ecosystem constitute both means and ends. This reform approach would require:

1. An overarching vision and set of purposes that speak to all young people, their parents, educators and wider social partners, and that provide the 'cultural glue' of the ecosystem.
2. A unified curriculum, assessment and qualifications framework for enhanced general and vocational education.
3. A more supportive and engaged role for employers and higher education providers, which would involve greater regulation of the labour market and a move towards the concept of a social partnership.
4. A strongly collaborative local learning system of providers that combines institutional autonomy with a strong sense of shared professionalism, locality and region, and is capable of supporting 14+ participation, progression and transition for all learners in an area.
5. A gradual and more deliberative policy process in which national leadership is focused more on providing a framework for professional and economic action at the local and regional levels and less on political micromanagement.

1. A common philosophy and sense of purpose – the glue of a new English system

The Nuffield Review of 14–19 Education and Training in England and Wales noted the relative absence of a set of broader aims and purposes for upper secondary education due to a narrow focus on attainment, the adoption of managerial language and what it considered to be the false dualisms of academic/vocational and ends/means.[70] It posed an overarching question for the 14–19 phase: 'What counts as an educated 19-year-old in this day and age?' To be an educated person, the Review suggested, requires intellectual development, practical capability, the capacity for full democratic and community participation, a commitment to moral seriousness and the pursuit of excellence and self-awareness. We are not suggesting that this is the last word on a set of common aims and purposes that can be applied to all 14–19-year-olds, but it is a good start. We could add a range of broader education system aims – the inclusion of all learners; stakeholders working together; a focus on sustainability, innovation and creativity; and a positive relationship between upper secondary education, the economy and wider democratic society. The issue is not so much what is on the list, but the need to actively debate and consider the overarching purposes of the system.

More specifically, we would suggest that all 14–19-year-olds undertake a balance of general and vocational activity in upper secondary education that will enable them to see themselves as both preparing for and playing an important role in their locality and wider society. Therefore, regardless of their specialisation, they would share certain common experiences, be empowered to ask the 'big questions' and contribute towards the building of what has been termed the 'good society'.[71] At its deepest, this particular concept of unification is associated with the human condition and the ability to relate thinking and doing.

2. Enhancing general and vocational education together – a unified baccalaureate approach

The purpose of the curriculum should sit at the centre of upper secondary education. Qualifications and their assessment need to be constructed in a way that supports the curriculum, thus the argument for a baccalaureate-style award that has a close alignment with a whole-curriculum approach. We argue that if we add to this the idea that general education should involve applied learning and that vocational education should involve theorisation, we create the case not only for a baccalaureate, but also for a unified baccalaureate approach.

A *British Baccalaureate,* published in 1990,[72] was the first unified baccalaureate blueprint and suggested that both general and vocational qualifications suffered from narrowness and should be reformed together within a single framework. What emerged thereafter were a number of proposals for unified baccalaureate models usually comprising a common core of learning, supplemented by subject specialisations. The precise design of these models varied – some emphasised a relatively large amount of common learning (including, for example, a modern foreign language), others less;

some were more prescriptive, stressing the need for particular combinations of subjects, while others promoted modular flexibility; some were more inclusive, comprising levels from Entry upwards, others less so; and some functioned more like a curriculum framework than a national qualification.[73] What they had in common was a whole-curriculum approach that attempted to balance breadth of learning and specialisation that could be applied to enhance both general and vocational education.

The policy moment for the core/specialisation model came in 2003 when designs derived from our English baccalaureate system[74] formed the centre of the Tomlinson unified Diploma system proposal.[75] Despite the fact that it did not become policy, it was widely praised as a sensible way of broadening A Levels and of bringing vocational learning to the centre of the 14–19 curriculum while attempting to include all learners.[76]

Since 2005 new factors have emerged that need to be taken into account, including the election of the Coalition Government. Arguably most serious of these is the Gove 'knowledge challenge'. The introduction of the English baccalaureate performance measure has put traditional subject knowledge at the centre of the debate because of the assertion that social inclusion will be assisted when young people from all social groups acquire what Michael Young refers to as 'powerful knowledge'.[77] We agree that this is an important argument, but the question is: how can all young people master knowledge from the established disciplines, and to what end?

We want to respond to the knowledge challenge by suggesting a four-fold reform of general education – first, promoting an idea of subjects that contain not only established knowledge but also the means to question that knowledge; second, the experience of different dimensions of general education, including a research project to encourage greater in-depth understanding and exploration of interdisciplinary knowledge; third, the opportunity to apply knowledge to life as it is experienced and to the major problems that face society; and, finally, an acceptance that an 'educated 19-year-old' requires the acquisition of and participation in different types of knowledge. These four proposals could be seen as extending our A Level academic tradition by developing a more 'connective specialisation' that reaches out beyond the boundaries of traditional subject knowledge to other forms of general and vocational education. However, we suggest that such reforms can only be achieved within a unified framework that overtly encourages this connectivity and also helps to produce a more expansive form of vocational education.

As part of the unified concept, we need to focus particularly on building a strong vocational education that functions as part of the 'mainstream', rather than as an 'alternative'; that is capable of attracting a wide range of young people; and that has a high degree of public understanding and confidence. Some have argued that vocational education can only achieve high status when it has its own separate track linked to the labour market and is part of a system of early specialisation in upper secondary education.[78] We have dealt with that argument earlier. Here we suggest that a strong vocational education needs to be both distinctive *and* integrated within a wider set of frameworks.

The most successful forms of vocational education in upper secondary systems (e.g. in Germany and the Nordic countries) underpin vocational skill and competence not only with vocational knowledge but also with general education.[79] This blend provides the vocational learner with the knowledge to be able to solve problems in the workplace, to understand the wider context within which the workplace operates, to be able to deliberate and judge, to be creative and to handle unpredictability. This combination of vocational and general education also creates the potential for the worker to become a lifelong learner and a more informed citizen.

The principle of underpinning vocational education with general education can also help us with the issue of specialisation and when it should begin. We are opposed to early vocational specialisation because, in the English system, this will result in educational and social segregation. At the same time, we support the idea of strong vocational futures. If vocational education is underpinned by general education, the result can be clear vocational routes within a common framework. Many young people prefer to learn in vocational settings. Our task is to ensure that in doing so they are able to progress to higher education as well as the workplace. Alison Fuller and Lorna Unwin have argued for a 'dual system' or 'alternance model' that combines general and vocational education and provides young people with an ability to progress and to change direction.[80] We would suggest that their concept of duality can be contained within the wider unified and universal upper secondary system being explored here.

Realising the potential of this blend of distinctiveness and commonality in vocational education will depend on four wider conditions – first, an upper secondary curriculum that offers opportunities to apply general education knowledge to real vocational situations; second, the provision of industry-standard facilities and well-trained staff; third, the development of high-quality apprenticeships on a scale that alters public perceptions of vocational opportunity; and fourth, workplaces that are prepared to utilise the skills and knowledge young people have acquired and to offer the possibility for more expansive work-based activity.[81] One defining feature of a strong vocational education is the number and quality of apprenticeships. In 2010 around 6 per cent of the 16–18 cohort in England was in an apprenticeship[82] and the quality of these programmes is highly variable.[83] Leading specialists on apprenticeships have concluded that a stronger national framework is required to develop their quality by, for example, promoting them at Level 4 and extending the licence to practise across a range of occupations. They also recommend that the policy of central targets should be abandoned and replaced by a more explicit social partnership approach at both national and local levels.[84]

3. A new, more supportive and engaged role for employers and higher education

Strong vocational education relies on specialist knowledge and skill fostered by expert institutions and professional communities of practice that have a close relationship with employers and employment. This is one of the lessons to be learnt from the Germanic and Nordic systems and their traditions of social partnership.[85] Forging these kind of 'alliances' within the English system has, however, been undermined by the weakness of incentives or frameworks for joint action and the strength of national policy levers (e.g. funding, qualifications and performance measures) that have pulled education and employers in different directions.[86] A full national system of social partnership will take decades to develop and would involve some difficult political decisions about the nature of the labour market and its regulation, but we could start locally. Here we suggest the formation of what we have called a 'devolved social partnership'[87] in which specialist vocational institutions, such as further education colleges, collaborate with vocational higher education providers, employer organisations and schools through regional and sub-regional networks. These would need power and resources from national government to bring partners together to collaborate around, for example, supporting young people to become entrepreneurs,[88] or around customising a national-based curriculum and qualifications to meet local needs. This final point is one that Alison Wolf[89] stressed in her report on 14–19 vocational education and was a well-regarded feature of BTEC qualifications in the late 1980s and early 1990s. Collaborative working of this type could also go some way towards tackling the problem of the lack of employers' recognition or regard for vocational qualifications and increasing understanding between employers and young people.

Higher education too will need to play its part in supporting the development of a universal upper secondary education system. As we have seen earlier, it has often had a constraining or even negative effect on 14–19 reform, but we would argue that it has the potential to make a positive contribution. Universities should be directly involved in the design and quality assurance of the unified baccalaureate system, and in recognising and building more actively on the knowledge and skills that young people acquire in the 14–19 phase. Many of the activities undertaken as part of the Aimhigher initiative provide a starting point for the kind of positive support higher education can offer.[90]

4. Collaboration and professionalism – a strong local approach

Education and training for 14–19-year-olds, while deeply influenced by national qualifications and policies on institutional arrangements (e.g. academies), is acted out at the local level. School sixth forms and colleges determine their own admissions criteria. Beyond 14, at some stage all learners (but lower attainers more often early on) will make a transition between institutions. Furthermore, improving choice of provision, particularly in the area of vocational education, depends on collaboration between schools, colleges and work-based learning providers. So the local really counts.

Reflecting on our work at institutional and local authority level over the last twenty years, we would suggest – somewhat counterintuitively – that a strong local approach to support the participation, progression and transition of *all* 14–19-year-olds in a locality will depend on strong national frameworks. By this we are referring to the need to reinforce local vision and voluntary collaborative working with a set of frameworks that makes it easier to achieve an active consensus and to bring everyone to the table. This is not about micromanaging from the centre, but about providing social partners in localities with parameters within which equity is assured and in which they have the space to exercise local discretion. This is what Lawrence Pratchett refers to as the 'freedom'[91] to bring about real, meaningful change in any particular area.

Elsewhere we have argued for a form of localism – 'democratic localism' – that involves rebalancing the state away from the centre and towards the local, with a new type of national leadership that offers direction without micromanagement, promotes a strong concept of the economic region and fosters a more collective sense of responsibility within and for the locality.[92] In practice, for example, this could mean that a national baccalaureate qualification could be made more locally relevant by providing local partnerships with the discretion to create locally adapted modules. These partnerships could also be strengthened by the creation of an 'area-based validation model' in which awarding bodies recognise the partnership as a vital basis of quality assurance. In addition, a framework approach would involve strengthening the commitment of autonomous institutions to the locality in order to improve the curriculum offer for all learners and to bring employers and universities together to ease 18+ transitions into higher education and the labour market. A number of local initiatives are already exploring how to develop stronger area-based approaches to respond to the current economic and policy climate. These include the formation of '14+ progression and transition boards' to more effectively integrate 14–19 partnerships, the community and the local labour market;[93] an 'area-based curriculum' that cements a closer relationship between learners, their immediate environment and their learning;[94] and further education colleges that act as hubs of local ecosystems of economic and social value creation.[95] These initiatives can benefit all young people, but particularly those who do not take a traditional academic route.

Central to the idea of the strong area and democratic localism is an enhanced concept of professionalism that means that teachers and lecturers have regard for all the learners in an area and not just the ones in their own institution. Here we are arguing for professionals to acquire more than one identity and to become both a specialist in terms of knowledge and skill and an educationist with understanding, empathy and commitment to an institution and to the locality. These identities encourage the teacher, tutor or manager not only to care for their own but also to look beyond the confines of their institution, to draw on community resources and to take a genuine interest in all young people across their local area. This is the first and most fundamental step to restraining the negative aspects of institutional autonomy and competition and to forming the new 'communities of practice'[96] required for a more unified, comprehensive and inclusive concept of upper secondary education.

But what kind of local leadership can bring all the pieces together? Here we come to refashioning the role of local authorities. They would be seen not as representatives of the bureaucratic state, but as the civic champions of the locality, a function they have undertaken in the past, but which has declined under new public management.[97] In this role local authorities would be orchestrators of multi-agency working and would offer independent leadership for collaboration between schools, colleges and work-based learning providers that would serve everyone within their area. This would mean reinvesting in local authorities' economic and political powers.

5. A slower and more inclusive policy process

Policy is not just about its content but also about how it is made and enacted.[98] Policy that is made quickly and is imposed from the centre has proved remarkably ineffective. It is expensive in terms of bureaucratic accountability and transaction costs, is prone to serious error and produces unintended outcomes because the conditions on the ground are far more complex than central policymakers appreciate. As Lawrence Angus reminds us, 'education is, first and foremost, a relational (and certainly not a managerial) enterprise'.[99]

There are very strong arguments for a different style of policy process in which democratically elected politicians set the general tone (although even here there is a case for a stronger social partnership approach to gain consensus) and leave spaces for its mediation at the lower levels, confident in the knowledge that those on the ground are better informed. However, this means getting beyond the double speak of devolution where politicians pretend to give autonomy to localities and institutions but retain the powerful policy levers in their own hands. In the new model, these too will have to be devolved, acting, as we have suggested earlier, as 'policy frameworks' that invite professional and popular participation. It is difficult to see a high-opportunity-progression ecosystem emerging without these changes to 'policy style', because what is needed is a new stability where change is slowed down so that everyone can deliberate and everything can adapt and evolve.

We see these five components working in synergy so that the leading role of the curriculum is informed by strong values and purposes, which together shape the qualifications that young people need to acquire; organisational arrangements in localities are constructed to maximise participation, progression and successful transition for young people; employers and higher education providers play a positive role in this critical phase; and national policy and the funding it offers creates the space within which all social partners collaborate for the benefit of 100 per cent of learners in a locality and the realisation of a universal upper secondary system.

Working for sustainable change

While we recognise the truth of Basil Bernstein's dictum that education cannot compensate for society,[100] as Lawrence Angus, writing about the system in Australia, asserts:

> *Educators cannot wait for widespread social, economic and political reform that will result in a more democratic society in which social justice and equality will prevail. We must keep chipping away at the greater goal of achieving democratic schooling for social justice.*[101]

It is in this spirit that we conclude the lecture. We have noted how the upper secondary phase in England is still in a process of formation with no clear consensus about its purpose, shape or future direction. As a result of its historical roots, the default setting has been selection rather than learner progression, and it is this that has produced the low-opportunity-progression equilibrium. Recent economic and policy developments appear only to be reinforcing this situation.

A universal upper secondary phase that promotes effective participation, progression and transition to higher study and employment for all learners – an essential educational goal in the twenty-first century – will, in our view, only be achieved when the culture of selection and division is addressed by an alliance of social and political partners to bring about sustainable change. This is why we have argued for the vision of a more unified approach to the 14–19 phase and a comprehensive ecosystem reform strategy that relates different policies, practices and structures, builds on historic strengths and directly addresses fundamental weaknesses.

This vision of a more unified universal upper secondary education system is not just our idea; it reflects various proposals for change by a wide range of social partners over the past two decades or more. The task of this lecture has been to crystallise this vision, to set it in the current economic and political context and to discuss the related dimensions of reform for its realisation.

We finish by asking one more question – What is it to be a public intellectual in this day and age? It certainly is about posing the most fundamental questions. At a time in which the Coalition Government seeks to turn back the clock, we are obliged to ask what education is for and, in particular, what the mission of upper secondary education is within this broader project?

However, our belief in a 'serious utopianism' requires consideration of practical strategies and of how we build an alliance within and beyond education.

We started out this evening by arguing for collaboration and we conclude by affirming its central role in bringing about sustainable change. A great deal of our twenty-year partnership has been spent working with a wide range of practitioners and policy-makers, as well as researchers, because of our belief in building inclusive alliances. We have led and contributed to networks that bring together different social partners – promoting a new generation of 14+ partnerships through the formation of 14+ progression and transition boards is but the latest example. A more connective and democratic way of working is a central feature of the ecosystem approach to the change advocated here.

We believe that the IOE, as a public university, is at its best when it applies its research and teaching expertise to a common enterprise in the service of all learners. The task we face in bringing about reform is too big for educationists alone because the crisis facing young people today requires reform that reaches into all parts of society. It is not enough to work towards a unified universal upper secondary education only to lead young people to the prospect of mass unemployment or a life with fewer opportunities than their parents enjoyed. The new economic and policy context we have described demands a greater partnership approach that is part of a much wider democratic, social and economic project. However, we know where our immediate responsibility lies. It is to secure the legitimacy of a *unified* and *universal* upper secondary system and to ensure that it has meaning for all young people, because they deserve a far better education and future than our current arrangements have been able to deliver thus far.

References

ACEVO (2012) Youth unemployment: the crisis we cannot afford. Online. <http://www.bristol.ac.uk/cmpo/publications/other/youthunemployment.pdf)> (accessed 17 February 2012).

Allen, M. and Ainley, P. (2012) Why young people can't get the jobs they want and the education they need. Online. <http://radicaled.wordpress.com/download-e-book-why-young-people-cant-get-the-jobs-they-want-and-the-education-they-need/> (accessed 20 April 2012).

Angus, L. (2012) 'Teaching within and against the circle of privilege: reforming teachers, reforming schools'. *Journal of Education Policy*, 27(2), 231–52.

Ball, S. (2008) *The Education Debate: Policy and politics in the 21st century*. Bristol: Policy Press.

Bernstein, B. (1970) 'Education cannot compensate for society'. *New Society*, 15(387), 344–7.

BIS (2012) *Post-16 Education and Skills: Learner participation, outcomes and level of highest qualification held*. Quarterly Statistical First Release. London: BIS.

Brown, P., Lauder, H. and Ashton, D. (2011) *The Global Auction: The broken promises of education, jobs and incomes*. Oxford: Oxford University Press.

Clarke, L. and Winch, C. (2007) *Vocational Education: International approaches, developments and systems*. London: Routledge.

Coffield, F., Edward, S., Finlay, I., Hodgson, A., Steer, R. and Spours, K. (2008) *Improving Learning, Skills and Inclusion: The impact of policy*. London: Routledge/Falmer.

Coffield, F. and Williamson, B. (2011) *From Exam Factories to Communities of Discovery: The democratic route*. London: Institute of Education, University of London.

Confederation of British Industry (CBI) (1989) *Towards a Skills Revolution*. London: CBI.

Couglan, S. (2012) UK university applications down as fees rise. BBC News, 30 January. Online. <http://www.bbc.co.uk/news/education-16787948> (accessed 13 March 2012).

De Waal, A. (2009) *Straight As? A level teachers' views on today's A levels*. London: Civitas.

Dearing, Sir R. (1996) *Review of Qualifications for 16–19 year olds*. London: SCAA.

DfE (2011a) The Education Act. Online. <http://www.education.gov.uk/aboutdfe/departmentalinformation/educationbill/a0073748/education-bill> (accessed 17 February 2012).

DfE (2011b) *Participation in Education, Training and Employment by 16–18 year olds in England*. Statistical First Release 15/2011. London: DfE.

DfES (2002) *14–19 Education: Extending opportunities, raising standards*. London: Stationery Office.

Dolphin, T. and Lanning, T. (2011) (eds) *Rethinking Apprenticeships*. London: IPPR.

Feinstein, L. (2003) 'Inequality in early cognitive development of British children in the 1970 cohort'. *Economica*, 70, 73–97.

Finegold, D. (1999) 'Creating self-sustaining, high-skill ecosystems'. *Oxford Review of Economic Policy*, 15(1), 60–81.

Finegold, D. and Soskice, D. (1988) 'The failure of training in Britain: analysis and prescription'. *Oxford Review of Economic Policy*, 4(3), 21–53.

Finegold, D., Keep, E., Miliband, D., Raffe, D., Spours, K. and Young, M. (1990) *A British Baccalaureate: Overcoming divisions between education and training*. London: IPPR.

Fuller, A. and Unwin, L. (2008) Towards expansive apprenticeships: a commentary by the Teaching and Learning Research Programme. Online. <http://www.tlrp.org/pub/documents/apprenticeshipcommentaryFINAL.pdf> (accessed 29 February 2012).

Fuller, A. and Unwin, L. (2011) 'Vocational education and training in the spotlight: back to the future for the UK's Coalition Government?'. *London Review of Education*, 9(2), 191–204.

Gazelle (2012) Enterprising futures: the changing landscape and new possibilities for further education. Online. <http://www.thegazellegroup.com/gazelle-publication.php> (accessed 20 April 2012).

Green, A. and Steedman, H. (1993) *Educational Provision, Educational Attainment and the Needs of Industry: A review of the research for Germany, France, Japan, the USA and Britain*. Report Series 5. London: National Institute of Economic and Social Research.

Hayward, G. and Williams, R. (2011) 'Joining the big society: Am I bothered?'. *London Review of Education*, 9(2), 175–90.

Higham, J. and Yeomans, D. (2007) 'Policy memory and policy amnesia in 14–19 education: learning from the past?'. In D. Raffe and K. Spours (eds), *Policy-making and Policy Learning in 14–19 Education*. London: Institute of Education, University of London.

Hodgson, A. and Spours, K. (2003a) *Beyond A Levels: Curriculum 2000 and the reform of 14–19 qualifications*. London: Kogan Page.

Hodgson, A. and Spours, K. (2003b) 'A baccalaureate system for the English context'. In G. Phillips and T. Pound (eds), *The Baccalaureate: A model for curriculum reform*. London: Kogan Page.

Hodgson, A. and Spours, K. (2007) 'Specialised diplomas: transforming the 14–19 landscape in England?'. *Journal of Education Policy*, 22(6), 657–73.

Hodgson, A. and Spours, K. (2008) *Education and Training 14–19: Curriculum, qualifications and organization*. London: Sage.

Hodgson, A. and Spours, K. (2009) Baccalaureates and curriculum frameworks in the English 14–19 system: A scoping paper for the Sixth Form Colleges Forum. Online. <http://www.ioe.ac.uk/Bacs_and_curriculum_frameworks_14-19.pdf> (accessed 28 February 2012).

Hodgson, A. and Spours, K. (2010) 'Vocational qualifications and progression to higher education: the case of the 14–19 Diplomas in the English system'. *Journal of Education and Work*, 23(2), 95–110.

Hodgson, A. and Spours, K. (2011a) 'Educating 14–19 year olds in England: a UK lens on possible futures'. *London Review of Education*, 9(2), 259–70.

Hodgson, A. and Spours, K. (2011b) 'National education systems: the wider context'. In A. Hodgson, K. Spours and M. Waring (eds), *Post-compulsory Education and Lifelong Learning across the United Kingdom: Policy, organisation and governance*. London: Institute of Education, University of London.

Hodgson, A. and Spours, K. (2012) 'Three versions of "localism": implications for upper secondary education and lifelong learning in the UK'. *Journal of Education Policy*, 27(2), 193–210.

Hodgson, A., Spours, K. and Waring, M. (2005) 'Higher education, Curriculum 2000 and the future reform of 14–19 qualifications in England'. *Oxford Review of Education*, 31(4), 479–95.

Keep, E. (2002) 'The future of the work-based route in England – The tethered beetle of policy takes another turn'. Public lecture at the Institute of Education, University of London, 23 February.

Keep, E. (2005) 'Reflections on the curious absence of employers, labour market incentives and labour market regulation in English 14–19 policy: first signs of a change of direction?'. *Journal of Education Policy*, 20(5), 533–53.

Keep, E. (2011) 'The English skills policy narrative'. In A. Hodgson, K. Spours and M. Waring (eds), *Post-compulsory Education and Lifelong Learning Across the United Kingdom: Policy, organisation and governance.* London: Institute of Education, University of London.

Keep, E. and James, S. (2012) 'A Bermuda triangle of policy? Bad jobs, skills policy and incentives to learn at the bottom end of the labour market'. *Journal of Education Policy*, 27(2), 211–30.

Labour Party (1996) *Aiming Higher: Labour's proposals for the reform of the 14–19 curriculum.* London: Labour Party.

Lave, J. and Wenger, E. (1991) *Situated Learning: Legitimate peripheral participation.* Cambridge: Cambridge University Press.

Lawson, N. and Spours, K. (2011) *Education for the Good Society.* London: Compass Publications.

Lea, R. (2004) 'We should develop a proper apprenticeship route from 14'. In C. Ryan (ed.), *Bac or Basics: Challenges for the 14–19 curriculum.* London: Social Market Foundation, 34–7.

Learning and Skills Council (LSC) (2008) National Learner Satisfaction Survey 2007. Online. <http://readingroom.lsc.gov.uk/lsc/National/NLSS_Highlights_Report_final_July08.pdf> (accessed 17 February 2012).

London Youth (2011) *Hunch: A vision for youth in post-austerity Britain.* London: London Youth.

Lumby, J. and Foskett, N. (2005) *14–19 Education: Policy, leadership and learning.* London: Sage.

Macfarlane, E. (1993) *Education 16–19: In transition.* London: Routledge.

Newman, J. (2001) *Modernising Governance: New Labour, policy and society.* London: Sage/OUP.

OECD (2004) *Education at a Glance: OECD indicators.* Paris: OECD.

Office for National Statistics (ONS) (2012) Labour Market Statistics, February 2012. Online. <http://www.ons.gov.uk/ons/rel/lms/labour-market-statistics/february-2012/statistical-bulletin.html> (accessed 17 February 2012).

Passy, R. and Morris, M. (2010) *Evaluation of Aimhigher: Learner attainment and progression. Final report.* Bristol: HEFCE.

Perry, E. and Francis, B. (2010) *The Social Class Gap for Educational Achievement: A review of the literature.* London: RSA.

Plowright, D. and Barr, G. (2012) 'An integrated professionalism in further education: a time for phronesis?'. *Journal of Further and Higher Education*, 36(1), 1–16.

Poon Scott, E. (2011) 'The A Levels resit policy and its effects on student learning in three educational institutions in England'. Unpublished PhD thesis, University of Sussex, Brighton.

Pound, T. (2003) 'From Crowther to Curriculum 2000'. In G. Phillips and T. Pound (eds), *The Baccalaureate: A model for curriculum reform.* London: Kogan Page.

Pratchett, L. (2004) 'Local autonomy, local democracy and the "new localism"'. *Political Studies,* 52, 358–75.

Pring, R., Hayward, G., Hodgson, A., Johnson, J., Keep, E., Oancea, A., Rees, G., Spours, K. and Wilde, S. (2009) *Education for All: The future of education and training for 14–19 year olds.* London: Routledge.

Raffe, D. (1988) *Education and the Youth Labour Market: Schooling and scheming.* London: Routledge.

Raffe, D. and Spours, K. (2007) *Policymaking and Policy Learning in 14–19 Education.* London: Institute of Education, University of London.

Richardson, W. (2011) 'The weight of history: structures, patterns and legacies of secondary education in British Isles c. 1200–c. 1980'. *London Review of Education* 9(2), 153–74.

Ryan, C. (2004) 'Don't dumb down the baccalaureate'. In C. Ryan (ed.), *Bac or Basics: Challenges for the 14–19 curriculum.* London: Social Market Foundation, 64–73.

Spours, K., Stanton, G., Vesey, R. and West, J. (2012) *The Overlooked Middle: Becoming the new NEETs?* London: Centre for Post-14 Research and Innovation, Institute of Education, University of London.

Stanton, G. and Fletcher, M. (2006) '14–19 institutional arrangements in England: a research perspective on collaboration, competition and patterns of post-16 provision'. Nuffield Review Working Paper 38.

Thomas, L. (2011) Lessons for localism: the RSA area-based curriculum. Online. <http://www.thersa.org/__data/assets/pdf_file/0006/558150/RSA_Lessons-for-localism_report.pdf> (accessed 1 March 2012).

Tomlinson Report: see Working Group on 14–19 Reform (below).

Toynbee, P. (2012) 'These empty apprenticeship schemes are failing our young. Apprenticeships touted as solutions to the grave crisis of youth unemployment are not remotely up to the job'. *The Guardian*, 9 February, 36.

Truss, E. (2011) *Academic Rigour and Social Mobility: How low income students are being kept out of top jobs*. London: Centre Forum.

Wilde, S. and Wright, S. (2007) 'On the same wavelength but tuned to different frequencies? Perceptions of academic and administrative staff in England and Wales on the articulation between 14–19 education and training and higher education'. *London Review of Education* 5(3), 299–312.

Wolf, A. (2011) *Review of Vocational Education: The Wolf Report*. London: DfE.

Working Group on 14–19 Reform (2004) *14–19 Curriculum and Qualifications Reform: Final report of the Working Group*. London: DfES.

Young, M. (2009) 'What are schools for?' In H. Daniels, H. Lauder and J. Porter (eds), *Knowledge, Values and Educational Policy*. London: Routledge.

Notes

1 We use the term 'upper secondary education' to refer to the education of 14–19-year-olds in England. This is the term normally used in international literature for this phase of education, even though it is not extensively used in England.

2 It is important to note that we are only talking about England in this lecture and not the UK as a whole. As our article in the *London Review of Education* (Hodgson and Spours, 2011a) point outs, the education and training systems across the four countries of the UK are different and divergence is increasing.

3 Wolf Report, 2011; Hayward and Williams, 2011; Allen and Ainley, 2012.

4 Lawson and Spours, 2011.

5 Higham and Yeomans, 2007.

6 Pring *et al.*, 2009.

7 Coffield and Williamson, 2011.

8 DfES, 2002.

9 See London Youth, 2011, for a convincing argument on this point.

10 Lumby and Foskett, 2005.

11 Learning and Skills Council, 2008. Over 90 per cent of 16+ students in further education (this included sixth form colleges) were satisfied with their learning experience, with 27 per cent 'extremely satisfied', although the figures were higher for older learners.

12 Office for National Statistics, 2012; ACEVO, 2012.

13 Perhaps the exception was the Nuffield Review of 14–19 education and training in England and Wales (2003–2009).

14 Brown *et al.*, 2011.

15 Lawson and Spours, 2011.

16 For example, Feinstein, 2003.

17 OECD, 1994.

18 Green and Steedman, 1993.

19 Richardson, 2011.

20 Finegold and Soskice, 1988.

21 Allen and Ainley, 2012.

22 Spours *et al.*, 2012.

23 Plowright and Barr, 2012.

24 Keep, 2005, p. 533.

25 Ewart Keep in his public lecture 'The future of the work-based route in England – the tethered beetle of policy takes another turn', at the Institute of Education, University of London, 23 February 2002, used the concept of the 'tethered beetle' to describe policy on work-based learning in England. Here we use the same metaphor, but apply it to the 14–19 system as a whole.

26 Poon Scott, 2011.

27 Pring *et al.*, 2009; Coffield and Williamson, 2011.

28 Hodgson and Spours, 2007.

29 The English Baccalaureate (EBacc) is a new performance measure introduced in 2011. To reach this measure 16-year-olds need to get good GCSEs (grades A*–C) in English, Mathematics, Science, an ancient or modern foreign language other than English, and either History or Geography. The percentage of students gaining the EBacc has become one of the key indicators used to judge school performance.

30 Wolf, 2011.

31 Hodgson and Spours, 2011b.

32 Stanton and Fletcher, 2006.

33 Wolf, 2011; Toynbee, 2012.

34 Keep, 2011, argues that England focuses on supply-side policies in relation to skills, whereas Scotland has begun to make policy that is also based on skills utilisation. See also Keep and James, 2012.

35 Hodgson *et al.*, 2005; Hodgson and Spours, 2010.

36 Wilde and Wright, 2007.

37 Coffield *et al.*, 2008.

38 Angus, 2012.

39 Coffield and Williamson, 2011.

40 ACEVO, 2012.

41 Higham and Yeomans, 2007.

42 Pound, 2003.

43 Macfarlane, 1993.

44 Finegold *et al.*, 1990.

45 Dearing, 1996.

46 Hodgson and Spours, 2008.

47 Hodgson and Spours, 2003a.

48 Labour Party, 1996.

49 Hodgson *et al.*, 2005.

50 For example, De Waal, 2009.

51 The 14–19 Diplomas were introduced as the government's response to the Tomlinson Report in 2004. Originally called 'Specialised Diplomas', they covered broad sectoral areas (e.g. Engineering, Business administration and finance, Creative and media) and there were a total of 14 'Lines of Learning', which were to be gradually introduced between 2008 and 2010. They were introduced to sit alongside GCSEs/A Levels, Apprenticeships and Foundation Learning as one of the four major progression routes for 14–19-year-olds. Situated in this 'middle ground' as broad vocational qualifications they thus did not follow the recommendations in the Tomlinson Report that the Diploma system should subsume all forms of learning for 14–19-year-olds. In response to criticisms that they only catered for learners wanting vocational courses, there was a proposal by then Secretary of State Ed Balls, who was a very strong supporter of the Diplomas, that they should be joined by three general education Diplomas in science, languages and humanities. These latter Diplomas were scrapped at the design phase by the incoming Coalition Government in 2010. The 14 Lines of 14–19 Diplomas were ill-fated from the start, despite the large sums of money spent on their design, implementation and promotion, and never achieved critical mass in terms of learner numbers. (See Hodgson and Spours, 2008, for more detail.)

52 The AQA Bacc is a Level 3 award, developed by the AQA examination board, which was first piloted in 2008 and is focused on application for university, with over 100 centres involved by 2009. It comprises four main components: Specialist depth of study – three A Levels of the student's choice; Independent learning – an extended project; Personal development – enrichment activities (two of three areas from work-related learning,

community participation and personal development) totalling a minimum of 100 hours and recorded in the AQA enrichment diary; Breadth – a minimum of an AS Level in General Studies, Critical Thinking or Citizenship.

53 The SFBac, which was designed and promoted by the Sixth Form Colleges Forum, is a curriculum and certification framework to highlight the learning experience of students in sixth form colleges, which promotes 'subjects, skills, values, breadth'. The SFBac is intended to provide an assurance that sixth form college students come out of secondary education with more than just qualifications and will be prepared for continuing education, life, work and citizenship.

54 The Extended Project Qualification (EPQ) can be taken at Levels 2 and 3 and provides students with the opportunity to develop and demonstrate research, independent learning and presentation skills. The student decides a topic for study and is normally guided by a supervisor/tutor towards accreditation rather than attending a course of study. The EPQ was originally built into the design of the 14–19 Diplomas and was a compulsory part of the accreditation framework. With the demise of the Diplomas it is now primarily taken as a free-standing qualification alongside a student's programme of GCSEs, A Levels or broad vocational qualifications. It has UCAS tariff points attached to it and is often used as part of the portfolio of qualifications offered by Advanced Level students for entry to higher education.

55 MP Elizabeth Truss, writing for the think tank Centre Forum in March 2011, proposed the development of an A Level Baccalaureate comprising at least three 'academic' A Levels, an AS in Mathematics and an AS in humanities or languages. See Truss, 2011.

56 Raffe, 1988.

57 DfE, 2011a.

58 Coughlan, 2012.

59 Brown *et al.*, 2011.

60 Coffield and Williamson, 2011.

61 Wolf, 2011.

62 Studio schools are designed for 14–19-year-olds of all abilities. They are small schools for 300 students. In order to provide a work-like environment, they are open all year, have a 9–5 working day, and include teaching through enterprise projects and real work. Studio schools offer a range of academic and vocational qualifications, including GCSEs in English, Maths and Science, as well as paid work placements linked directly to employment opportunities in the local area. The first studio school was opened in September 2010.

63 A university technical college (UTC) is a new type of school for 14–19-year-olds, which specialises in technical studies and is sponsored by a university. Each UTC will have two specialisms: the JCB Academy in Staffordshire, for example – the first UTC to open – specialises in engineering and construction. It offers full-time courses that combine practical and academic studies, so that from the ages of 14–16 learners will spend approximately 60 per cent of their time undertaking general education certificated through GCSEs and the other 40 per cent taking more specialised and technical qualifications related to a particular sector. These proportions will be reversed for

16–19-year-olds who will be able to specialise for 60 per cent of their time. In order to accommodate this broader curriculum, the UTCs have an extended school day, which runs from 8.30–5.30. Students are expected to progress either to apprenticeships, higher education or employment when they complete their studies.

64 Keep and James, 2012.

65 Perry and Francis, 2010.

66 Keep and James, 2012, p. 218.

67 Dual system ideas for English education were promoted by, for example, the Confederation of British Industry (CBI), 1989.

68 Wolf, 2011.

69 Finegold, 1999.

70 Pring *et al.*, 2009, pp. 14–18.

71 Lawson and Spours, 2011; Coffield and Williamson, 2011.

72 Finegold *et al.*, 1990.

73 Hodgson and Spours, 2009.

74 Hodgson and Spours, 2003b .

75 Working Group on 14–19 Reform, 2004.

76 This inclusive approach to a 14–19 Diploma system, which provides accreditation at four levels from Entry to Advanced in order to include all 14–19-year-olds, has not been replicated in any other official Diploma or Baccalaureate models.

77 Young, 2009.

78 For example, Ryan, 2004; Lea, 2004.

79 For example, Clarke and Winch, 2007.

80 Fuller and Unwin, 2011.

81 See Fuller and Unwin, 2008, for a discussion of the features of 'restrictive' and 'expansive' workplaces and how they can make a difference to the experience of apprenticeship.

82 Apprenticeship figures are notoriously difficult to track down and understand. This figure comes from DfE, 2011b (see also BIS, 2012), and it is not clear whether these learners are in colleges or in the workplace – the term 'apprenticeship' appears to be used somewhat loosely. Certainly the figure is under 10 per cent.

83 Fuller and Unwin, 2011; Dolphin and Lanning, 2011.

84 Dolphin and Lanning, 2011.

85 Clarke and Winch, 2007.

86 Keep and James, 2012.

87 See the final chapter of Coffield *et al.*, 2008, and Hodgson and Spours, 2012, for a longer discussion of this approach.

88 Gazelle, 2012.

89 Wolf, 2011.

90 See the evaluation of the Aimhigher programme in Passy and Morris, 2010.

91 Pratchett, 2004.

92 Hodgson and Spours, 2012.

93 The concept of 14+ progression and transition boards (14+ PTBs) has been developed at the Centre for Post-14 Research and Innovation (see http://www.ioe.ac.uk/research/165.html) at the IOE. A 14+ PTB, as its name implies, has the prime aim of promoting the progression of young people both within the education and training system and in their transition to the labour market, apprenticeship, further and higher education. This extended notion of progression leads to the term '14+' rather than just '14–19'. Moving to more vertically integrated arrangements around progression and transition, PTBs involve a wide range of education and training institutions, employer organisations, local and regional regeneration agencies, voluntary and community organisations and local authority support services for young people. The first 14+ PTB was set up in a local authority area in the East Midlands in 2011 (see http://www.ioe.ac.uk/research/49007.html) and several other local authority areas have become interested in following their example.

94 See Thomas, 2011, for an English example; see Angus, 2012, for similar ideas in the Australian context.

95 Gazelle, 2012.

96 The term 'community of practice' was originally coined by Lave and Wenger, 1991.

97 Newman, 2001.

98 Raffe and Spours, 2007, and Ball, 2008.

99 Angus, 2012, p. 245.

100 Bernstein, 1970.

101 Angus, 2012, p. 247.

Pour tous les enfants et les enseignants de l'Institut International de Lancy (Genève) et pour toutes les classes qui partiront en Angleterre !

Moi, à leur place, je serais comme ça !

Génial ! Mon école part...

EN VOYAGE À LONDRES

Laurent Audouin

Les P'tits Bérets

Dimanche 4 mai, 19 heures :

Demain, c'est LE grand jour,
ou plutôt THE BIG DAY !
Avec ma classe,
nous partons en voyage scolaire à Londres !
Eh oui… Vous avez bien entendu :
direction LONDON !

Yes, double Yes, triple Yes !

Et cette fois, la classe de Pierre, mon « pénible de frère »,
ne nous accompagne pas.
Normal, ils sont en CE2 et ils ne parlent pas assez bien anglais,
alors ça servirait à rien.

Et puis, dans deux ans, ce sera à son tour,
alors il peut bien attendre encore un peu.

Important Ah, j'allais oublier : nous partons en avion !
Quadruple Yes !

Avec ma mère, c'est toujours pareil : que je parte un jour ou une semaine, ma valise est toujours pleine à craquer !

J'appelle ça la valise « Au cas où… ».
Au cas où il pleuvrait, il neigerait,
il y aurait trop de soleil, trop de vent,
voire un tsunami, un tremblement de terre,
une invasion extraterrestre.
Bref, au cas où, elle pense à tout.

Maman, il me faut une place
pour les souvenirs à rapporter : c'est VITAL !

Il faut quand même que je vous donne le programme :

* Visite du Musée Roald Dahl
(celui qui a écrit Charlie et la chocolaterie)
* Le London Eye
(la grande roue de Londres)

* Croisière sur la Tamise
* Windsor Castle (cool)
(le château de la Reine)

* Chez Madame Tussauds
(le musée des célébrités en cire)
* Visite des studios Harry Potter
(où on a tourné ses films)

Ça promet une super belle semaine !

Bon, ce qui est moins drôle,
c'est qu'on aura des cours d'anglais tous les matins…

(Oh my God !)

Et j'aurai de l'argent de poche :

Pur plaisir !
(Hmm)

Finalement, Pierre, il est plein de bon sens !

20 h 30 : « Les enfants, au lit.
21 h 30 : Mathilde… il faut éteindre.
22 h 30 : Mathilde… il faut dormir.
23 h 30 : Mathilde… il faut dormir.

Mathilde, je te rappelle qu'on a rendez-vous demain matin à 8 h 15 à l'aéroport… Alors maintenant IL FAUT DORMIR ! »
Houlala, je sens que la nuit va être longue… Pff !

Lundi 5 mai, 7 h 40 : direction l'aéroport !

Allez, un bisou et mille milliards de recommandations… Et c'est parti !

8 h 15 : pile à l'heure devant le comptoir de la compagnie aérienne et je retrouve mes copains et copines (encore plus à l'heure que moi). Younès s'est fait un nouveau look avec une drôle de couleur dans les cheveux : une crête frisée blonde. Visiblement ça plaît à Olivia.

Emma et Solveig (ça se prononce « Soulevaille », parce qu'elle est franco-norvégienne) sont là aussi !

Pendant qu'on se retrouve, les enseignants sont assaillis par nos parents, avec des questions plein la bouche :

« Ah, il est temps d'embarquer ! » Ouf…
C'est la phrase magique qui sauve M. Gomu !
On laisse nos familles de l'autre côté de la vitre… Re-ouf !
Il ne reste que le passage obligatoire de la douane avant de monter dans l'avion.

À la sécurité de l'aéroport :

on doit déposer toutes nos affaires en métal dans un casier : appareil photo, ceinture, pièces de monnaie, Ipod, MP3… Bref, c'est l'inspection totale !

On doit aussi finir nos bouteilles pour les mettre à la poubelle. C'est pire qu'à la cantine quand on doit finir nos assiettes.

10 h 15 : on décolle enfin !

Le vol dure une heure et demie... Ça va vite.
Comment te sens-tu, Younès ? D'habitude il a le mal des transports.

« Impec ! Par contre, j'ai les oreilles bouchées !.
J'entends plus rien. »

Pour les oreilles, il y a une technique : un *chewing-gum* !
Mâche, mâche, mâche... Ça va te les déboucher !

« Comment ? Hein ? Quoi ? Qu'est-ce que tu dis ? »

Midi : arrivée à Londres ! Nous nous précipitons vers le tapis à bagages.

C'est la pagaille, on crie, on s'excite, hahaha !
Madame Forel intervient… fortement !

C'est boooon ? On peut y aller ? … Merci !

Valises sous les bras,
nous montons dans le bus,
direction le terminus : la pension anglaise !

13 h 30 : nous déposons, ou plutôt nous jetons nos bagages dans les chambres avant de filer au réfectoire pour notre premier repas anglais ! On meurt de faim !

Trop *cool*, c'est un *self* ! On peut prendre ce que l'on veut ! Normalement avec nos parents, c'est cinq fruits et légumes par jour… Mais là, finis les bons principes !

En plus de ça, on a même le droit de se resservir ! Les garçons font le concours de la plus grosse assiette et Younès a la révélation de la cuisine *made in England* :

Hmm, c'est trop bon les beans !

Après le déjeuner, nous rencontrons nos professeurs d'anglais, qui seront aussi nos guides pendant le séjour.

Désormais, quand nous serons avec eux, nous devrons parler en anglais, rien qu'en anglais, exclusivement en anglais… *Only in English*!

Glaups!

Allez, en route pour notre première visite :

15 h 05 : le musée de Roald Dahl (à Great Missenden)...

Nous sommes en pleine campagne anglaise, dans un petit village.
Le musée est minuscule : c'est juste la maison de l'auteur.

Dedans, on voit son fauteuil de travail, son bureau et toute sa vie…
expliquée en anglais ! Arghh, pas fastoche à comprendre.

Bon, je vous résume :

Et un de ses personnages célèbres :

Le meilleur moment, c'est LA BOUTIQUE,
pour notre premier shopping du voyage !

Je sais, ces souvenirs ne sont pas typiques de Londres, mais qu'est ce qu'on se marre dans cette boutique-souvenirs !

Avant de repartir, nous faisons un détour par le cimetière du village pour voir la tombe du célèbre auteur. Normalement, c'est silence obligatoire, mais les garçons (Younès en tête) font un peu les idiots et courent partout jusqu'à ce qu'ils découvrent la tombe d'un joueur de foot amateur.

18h30 : retour à la pension.

Nous avons une heure de libre pour discuter dans les chambres, ou envoyer un mot aux parents, ou faire un foot, ou juste se reposer. Ensuite, direction la douche avant de se retrouver au réfectoire. Je ne vous explique pas le menu, vous connaissez déjà : c'est *potatoes, sausage, baked beans* et compagnie. Par contre, niveau ambiance sonore, c'est le top.

Bref... C'est vraiment « la foire », comme dirait M. Gomu.

Mardi 6 mai :

Ce matin, au petit-déjeuner, Younès continue…

ses expériences culinaires et en découvre les conséquences !

9h05 : l'heure du premier cours d'anglais, en petits groupes. Euh… Monsieur Iain, comment fait-on si on ne comprend rien ?

« Yes… But it is not fastoche »

Je ne m'attendais pas à des cours comme cela :
nous commençons par le jeu du baccalauréat. C'est super rigolo !
Il faut trouver des mots en anglais à partir d'une lettre de l'alphabet.

Enfin, avec les copines on trouvait ça rigolo,
jusqu'à ce que les garçons se mettent à tricher,
juste pour nous embêter.
Que ce soit en français ou en anglais,
ils sont toujours les mêmes.

Iain reste calme

(On appelle ça le flegme britannique !)

À midi, nous nous retrouvons tous au réfectoire pour le déjeuner… Surtout pour se raconter cette première matinée de cours. Nous sommes tous d'accord : au début, ça nous barbait d'y aller, mais finalement, nous adorons apprendre l'anglais comme ça !

À la table de M. Gomu, ça discute beaucoup aussi. Il raconte que depuis hier soir, il passe son temps à répondre aux messages des parents. Visiblement, « ses devoirs » sont moins drôles que les nôtres !

À la fin du repas, M. Gomu sonne le rassemblement !
« Vous avez cinq minutes pour prendre vos affaires dans vos chambres :
un pull et un vêtement de pluie
car la météo prévue pour cet après-midi n'est pas terrible.
Et bien sûr, n'oubliez pas votre argent de poche s'il vous en reste.
Prenez aussi deux minutes pour vous brosser les dents ! »

Pas une seconde à perdre… On file et on se dépêche de revenir !
Pas étonnant ! Je vous rappelle le programme :

En arrivant dans le centre de Londres, ce qui nous frappe le plus, c'est le nombre de bus rouges ! Il y en a partout : c'est incroyable !

« Waouh, un bus de Londres ! Un autre bus de Londres… Waouh ! Et là, un bus de Londres… Et encore un bus de Londres… Et là, *one more* ! »

Le chauffeur passe sur le pont de Westminster, tourne à gauche, et là…

Le London Eye :
Génial !

Et voilà les enfants : le *London Eye* ! Nous allons monter dans une capsule et faire le tour complet de la roue. Ce sera le *London Tour* !

Mais, avant cela… Nous allons faire le « LTT »

C'est quoi le « LTT » ?

Le « LTT », c'est le *London Toilets Tour*,
répond M. Gomu en rigolant !
Allez hop, passage obligé aux toilettes, parce qu'une fois là-haut,
ce sera trop tard…
Car je vous rappelle que le tour complet dure trente minutes.

Pff, on fait la queue pour aller aux toilettes…
Et encore plus la queue pour accéder à la roue.
Cinq minutes… Dix minutes… Vingt minutes…
C'est looooong !
Dire qu'il y a toutes ces boutiques de souvenirs juste à côté
et qu'on n'a même pas le droit d'y aller !

Mon ticket en souvenir !

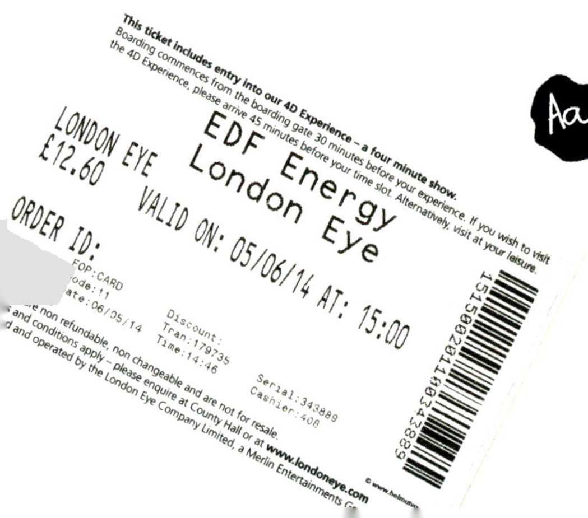

Ouf, ça y est… C'est à nous ! La porte de la capsule s'ouvre…
On se précipite à l'intérieur ! Et c'est parti !
Ça fait bizarre, on dirait qu'on n'avance pas et pourtant,
quinze minutes plus tard…

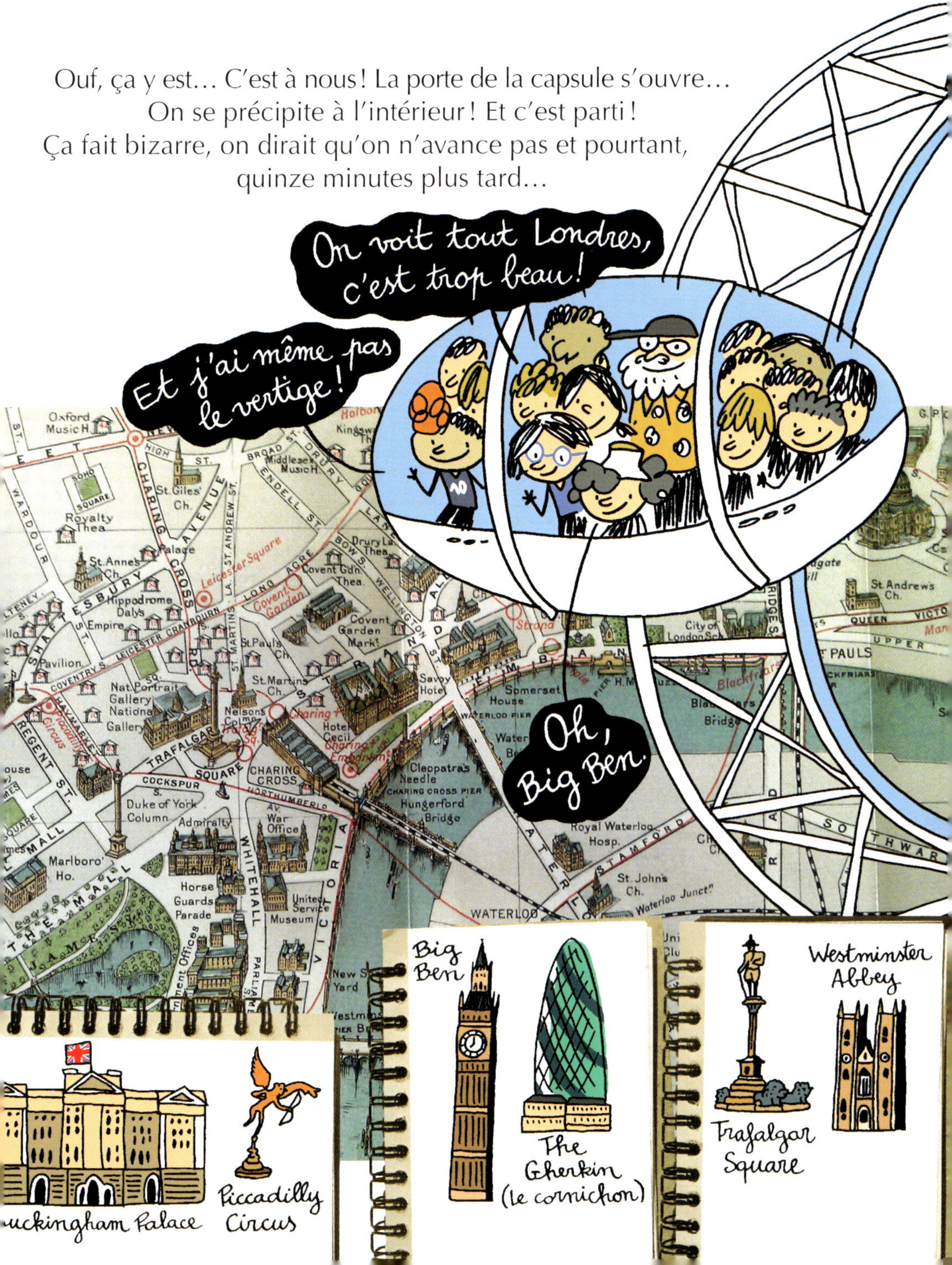

À la fin du tour, quand la porte de la capsule s'ouvre,
M. Gomu nous autorise à faire un tour dans les magasins de souvenirs.

C'est difficile de choisir LE cadeau en si peu de temps, surtout qu'il y a des milliards d'objets !

Ceci dit, au prix où ils vendent les souvenirs, le choix se fait assez vite ! C'est méga cher ! Après deux cartes, un magnet, un tee-shirt, mon budget est diminué de moitié ! Gloups !

Les garçons s'achètent tous une casquette, sauf Younès qui s'offre le super *sweat* à capuche !

16 h 30 : embarquement pour une mini-croisière sur la Tamise ! Même pas besoin de marcher puisque l'embarcadère est juste à côté du London Eye.

Une guide nous commente la visite en anglais, mais je n'y comprends rien. De toute façon, on n'écoute pas trop… On discute entre nous.

Ah si… Lui, je le reconnais !

M. Gomu avait raison au sujet de la météo !
Une goutte, puis deux, puis une belle averse ! Viiiite, à l'abri !
Nous filons tous à l'intérieur du bateau…
Sauf les garçons qui jouent les durs !

18h30 : c'est la fin de la balade pluvieuse en bateau. On se dépêche de remonter dans le bus.

Quand on sera de retour au centre ce sera l'heure de la douche !
« Les garçons… Je crois que M. Gomu avait demandé de prendre un vêtement de pluie, non ? »

20h10 : l'heure du dîner !

Le cuisinier, c'est le roi de la pomme de terre : il la cuisine à chaque repas avec beaucoup d'imagination !

Et même les « jacket potatoes » (avec des beans dedans)

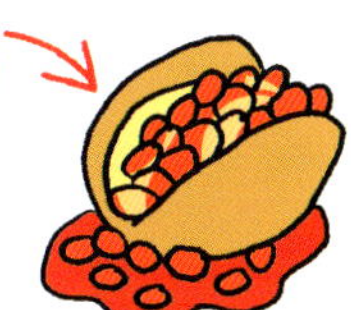

De retour dans nos chambres, on s'installe tranquillement pour faire des jeux ou discuter, mais M. Gomu frappe à toutes les portes.

« Oh non, M'sieur… On était en train de commencer une partie.
- Nous aussi, Monsieur… On vient juste de distribuer les cartes.
- Grmmmmm… Il n'y en a pas un de disponible ?
Et toi, Younès, tu fais quoi ?

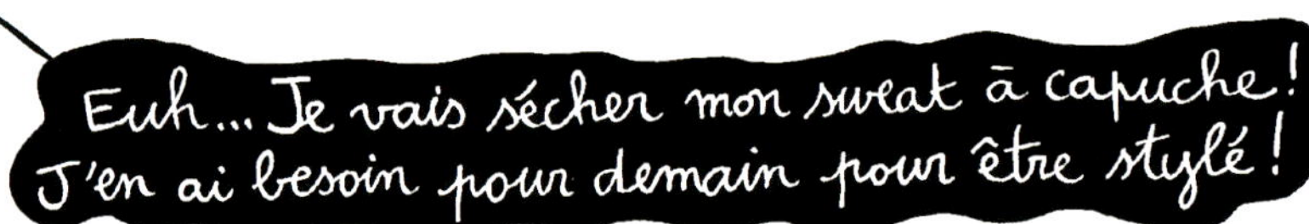

- Ah, c'est parfait ! Ton vêtement n'a pas besoin de toi pour sécher. Aller hop, tu le mets sur le radiateur et tu me suis. Solveig, tu viens aussi ! Toi qui as une famille « plutôt *high-tech* », tu seras la personne idéale pour envoyer les e-mails. »

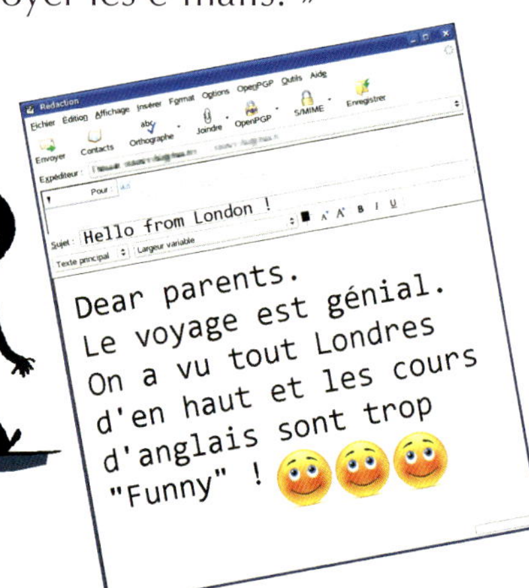
Sujet : Hello from London !

Dear parents.
Le voyage est génial.
On a vu tout Londres d'en haut et les cours d'anglais sont trop "Funny" !

Mercredi 7 mai : un bon petit-déjeuner (comme dirait Younès) pour bien démarrer la journée !

9 h 05 : nouvelle matinée, nouveau cours d'anglais ! Celui d'hier était amusant, mais celui d'aujourd'hui promet d'être encore plus sympa ! Iain et Diana nous attendent pour cuisiner !

Ariou Wraidi toucouc ?

Qu'est-ce que ça veut dire, déjà ?

T'inquiète, Mathilde, rappelle-toi : **Let's have fun !**

Nous allons préparer des *cupcakes* et un *sponge cake*, c'est-à-dire des gâteaux dans des petits moules en papier et un gâteau moelleux comme une éponge. Ça paraît compliqué à faire, nous ne sommes pas des pâtissiers !

Don't panic, it is very simple !

(Ah, ça, j'ai compris du premier coup… Je deviens bilingue !)

En vérité, c'est super fastoche :
il suffit d'ouvrir le sachet, de le verser dans un saladier
et de rajouter deux œufs… Et hop, ensuite on fait cuire !

Le plus compliqué, c'est d'arriver à ouvrir le sachet !

Oui, bon… J'exagère un peu, parce que le plus dur
c'était quand même de comprendre la recette en anglais !
Nous avons appris plein de nouveaux mots : *egg, bowl, to pour, to open…*
Maintenant, je peux le dire, je sais cuisiner à l'anglaise.

12 h 15 : à la cantine...

« Pourquoi ? Eh bien, parce que cet après-midi,
nous allons visiter le château de la Reine et qu'il faut savoir se tenir !
Il faut un peu varier ton alimentation anglaise,
sinon on va t'appeler Mister Bean ou Mitraillette Younès ! »

Nous avalons le repas rapidement et sans perdre de temps,
nous montons dans le bus, direction Windsor Castle…
Ensuite, ce sera le musée de cire de Madame Tussauds ! Waouhooo !

14h03 : nous arrivons devant le plus grand
et le plus vieux château fort habité au monde !
Windsor castle !
J'espère pour la famille royale qui habite ici,
que les douches et les toilettes
ne datent pas du Moyen Âge quand même.
(Le château est juste à côté de Londres)
Windsor
London

Dès l'entrée, le personnel de l'accueil nous prête des audio guides pour avoir plein d'explications sur le château ! Génial, la visite peut commencer !

« Ah, c'est malin ! Si tu ne touchais pas à tous les boutons, tu n'aurais pas déréglé ton appareil ! » répond M. Gomu en grognant. Moi, je vais voir un guide ou un garde (je ne sais pas trop, mais vu son costume, il doit bien tout savoir) pour lui demander si la Reine est là, puisqu'un drapeau flotte en haut de la tour.

Il me répond que quand elle est là, le drapeau royal est hissé ! Là, c'est juste le drapeau anglais.

À l'intérieur du château de Windsor, nous visitons la chapelle Saint-Georges qui abrite les tombeaux des souverains anglais ! Je trouve ça vraiment impressionnant : c'est un peu comme si on changeait d'époque (même si c'est rempli de touristes) !

À la sortie, nous sommes tous intrigués par les vrais gardes anglais… Alors, on se précipite pour les voir de près !

Ils ont une drôle de façon de marcher. On dirait des automates !

Quand les gardes s'arrêtent de marcher, ils doivent rester immobiles.
On dirait des statues ! Ils n'ont plus le droit de bouger,
comme quand on joue à 1, 2, 3, soleil !
Et pourtant autour d'eux, ça n'arrête pas !
Tous les touristes se font prendre en photo en les collant,
en faisant de grands sourires ou des grimaces.

Moi, à leur place,
je serais comme ça !

On continue la visite en découvrant les appartements royaux !
Houlalalalala, c'est grandiose… Il n'y a pas d'autres mots !
Des lits majestueux, des fresques magnifiques aux plafonds,
des tableaux de rois, de la vaisselle tout en argent…
Franchement, si la Reine déménage, moi je veux bien habiter chez elle !

Avant de partir, on passe par la boutique,
mais cette fois on ne s'attarde pas.
C'est super méga cher ! Je comprends mieux
pourquoi c'est si beau chez la Reine.
Bye bye Queen Elizabeth !

16h15:
Mathilde ! Tu as déjà visité un musée de cire ?
Croxley Luxury
HA HA HA...
VRRR
Non, pourquoi ?
Alors, tu ne connais pas mes oreilles !

« Trop drôle ! »

My ticket
Madame Tussauds
LONDON
Nous sommes là !
Madame Tussauds

Le bus nous dépose devant le musée.
Gloups… Je n'ai jamais vu autant de monde dans une file d'attente !
On reste là, sans avancer, sans bouger !
C'est bien simple, les statues de cire, c'est nous ! C'est long…
C'est loooong, c'est… Oh, miracle : on finit quand même par entrer !

À l'intérieur, tout le monde se précipite pour se faire prendre en photo avec les stars (en cire) ! Ce qui est amusant, c'est que nos enseignants reconnaissent plein de vedettes que je ne connais même pas et ils nous disent : « Quoi ? Vous ne savez pas qui c'est celui-ci ? Et celui-là, vous n'avez pas vu un de ses films ? »

John Travolta ! James Stewart ! John Wayne ! Al Pacino !

Mais nous, on en connaît plein aussi… Et là, on les scotche !
Désolés, M. Gomu, nous ne sommes pas de la même génération, ha ha !

Génial…
Ça valait le coup
d'avoir attendu
aussi longtemps !

Nous n'avons pas vu la Reine
au château de Windsor,
mais nous avons réussi à nous faire
prendre en photo avec toute la famille
royale chez Madame Tussauds…
Ce n'est quand même pas si mal, non ?

19 h 10 : de retour à Chalfont, Iain nous attend, un ballon dans la main !

Cool, nous avons du temps
avant d'aller dîner !
D'habitude, je ne joue
JAMAIS au foot,
mais bon, là,
ce sera une exception !

De son côté, Younès et le groupe de ceux qui ne veulent pas salir leurs vêtements *London* discutent de la boum (obligatoire) de demain soir et de comment inviter une fille à danser.

« Les filles, vous serez volontaires !
- Oh noooon, Monsieur Gomu ! »

Jeudi 8 mai : pour cette dernière journée en Angleterre, nous visitons les studios de tournage des films d'Harry Potter, le sorcier ! Alors, Iain et Diana nous font un cours spécial sur ce thème !

Ha ha ha, Younès !
Si j'avais les mêmes pouvoirs qu'Harry Potter,
il y a longtemps que je t'aurais transformé
en crapaud !

14 h 30 : après le repas de midi, et environ trente minutes de bus, nous arrivons au musée Harry Potter !

C'est la GRANDE excitation !

Yeeeees ! Yeeeees !

« Houlala, houlala, on se calme, fait M. Gomu ! C'est immense ! La visite dure environ trois heures, alors je vous demande de rester en groupe et de ne pas courir partout ! Je n'ai pas envie de passer le reste de la journée à vous chercher ! Il y a tellement de monde que je risquerais même de ne jamais vous retrouver, ha ha ha… »

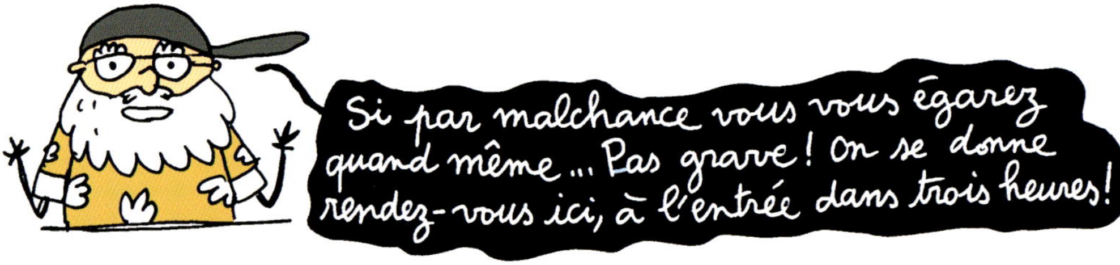

Une guide nous accueille et nous explique que tous les films du célèbre sorcier ont été tournés ici, et que nous allons découvrir les vrais décors des scènes et les vrais costumes des acteurs !
Alors là, je me rends compte qu'il y a deux sortes de visiteurs :

- ceux qui ne connaissent pas ou peu Harry Potter
- les fans : ceux qui savent tout sur tout et qui expliquent tout à tout le monde… en hurlant !

À savoir : les vrais fans, ça les agace si on ne sait pas tout comme eux ! Ils deviennent susceptibles.

C'est vraiment incroyable de se retrouver
dans de vrais studios de cinéma !
Je ne pensais pas qu'il y avait autant de choses à découvrir !
Il y a tellement de décors, de costumes, d'accessoires du film
que je ne sais même plus où regarder !

Sans oublier le décor principal des films : le château de Poudlard !
Ce n'est pas compliqué : il n'est pas géant...
Il est méga supra ultra géant ! C'est une maquette immmmmmmmense !
Je n'avais jamais vu un « faux château » aussi grand !

Alors bien sûr, après la visite (environ trois bonnes heures), nous nous retrouvons dans la boutique : tout nous fait envie !

On trouve quand même notre bonheur jusqu'au dernier centime de notre argent de poche !

18h45: retour à la pension et M. Gomu nous indique que juste après le dîner aura lieu… LA BOUM du dernier soir ! Donc, si l'on souhaite se préparer pour cette soirée, c'est maintenant !
Je ne sais pas si vous le savez, mais il y a trois façons de participer à une telle soirée :

1. décontracté : avec les mêmes habits de tous les jours !
2. local : avec les habits achetés lors du voyage !
3. chic : avec la tenue spéciale prévue avant le début du voyage !

Ensuite, le plus dur, c'est d'arriver à faire danser les garçons !

Quand toutes les boissons et les friandises ont été avalées, il n'y a plus d'excuse, cette fois il est temps d'aller sur la piste ! WOOOOOOoooOOOOHOUUUUUUUU !

C'est Iain qui fait le DJ et il connaît toutes les bonnes musiques ! On s'éclaaaaaaate de plus en plus à chaque nouveau morceau ! Et puis d'un coup... Tout s'arrête : le rythme, les paroles, les éclairages. Tout devient calme, les slows démarrent !

Olivia se précipite vers Younès.
Mme Forel invite M. Gomu.
Iain accepte l'invitation de Diana.
Bref, tout le monde suit le mouvement...

22h20 : fin de la boum... Et retour dans les chambres !

Vendredi 9 mai : cette fois, c'est le jour du départ.

Bye bye England ! *Bye bye* Iain, Diana et la Reine Elizabeth !

« Allez, ne traînons pas, fait M. Gomu…
Nous avons un avion à prendre et si nous le loupons,
je ne vous dis pas la tête de vos parents ! »

13h30 : c'est le décollage pour la France !

Retrouve toutes les aventures de Mathilde !

www.lesptitsberets.fr
Le blog de Mathilde : http://carnetdemathilde.canalblog.com/

Loi n°49-956 du 16 juillet 1949 sur les publications destinées à la jeunesse.
ISBN : 978-2-918194-46-0 - Dépôt légal : 3e trimestre 2014.
Achevé d'imprimer sur les presses de Grafiche AZ srl.